First published by AuthorHouse 04/07/04

ISBN: 1-4184-0713-5 (e)
ISBN: 1-4184-0649-X (sc)

Library of Congress Control Number: 2003098197

Printed in the United States of America
Bloomington, Indiana

This book is printed on acid-free paper.

LIST OF CONTENTS

GUIDE FOR MY SURVIVOR
© 2002

---- How to Assemble Guide into an Orderly Document.
---- Security and Safe Keeping of Documents.
---- Information For Annuitant.
---- How Can You Help Your Spouse, Family and Friends?
---- Personal Information.

---- Purpose.
---- Last Will and Testament.
---- Do You Need a Will?
---- Living Will.
---- Durable Powers of Attorney for Health Care.
---- Revocable Living Trust.
---- Do You Need a Revocable Living Trust?
---- Bypass Trust.
---- Death Certificate.

---- Purpose.
---- Notification List.
---- American Red Cross.
---- Notification by Mail.
---- Name and Address List.

To order additional copies of

Guide For My Survivor

By

Jose Pineda,

Call 1-888-280-7715

or

www.authorhouse.com

INTRODUCTION

© 2002

The author has written the Guide For My Survivor, to help people at all levels of life to prepare and annotate the current status of their personal affairs. To organize a file of instructions and to correlate (put together) for survivor or beneficiary those important documents into one binder, before his or her demise

It is not the intention of the author to offer any "legal" advice by any means. Annuitant must seek legal advice from their attorney, lawyer, and other legal advisors within their community, state and federal government officials.

The Guide For My Survivor - GFMS, is offered to the general public, civil service employees, all active and retired military personnel and their families. It is strongly recommended for all school students, elders and retiree annuitants at all levels of life and people married to foreign spouses.

This guide is published in paperback book for mailing and handling. You need to remove cover and pages from the binding to insert into document protectors. To accomplish the separation, cut <u>closely</u> along the binding with scissors or sharp instrument. The GFMS is also available via electronic books, refer to page-six to order paperback copies or through Internet downloading to your computer.

You will need a two or three-inch, three prong binder to accommodate your GFMS and documents. Label the outside of binder for positive identification with title and your name. Purchase heavyweight sheet protectors, 3.3 mills in thickness. Protectors must accommodate documents without making holes in documents and be bottom sealed to keep document from sliding out. Ask for acid free, non-glare material, archival safe, which won't lift print. The GFMS is a private document for life long use and must be protected with the best products. You will need a minimum of one-hundred (100) sheet protectors.

The GFMS offers individual people from the young to the elders at all levels of life, the opportunity to correlate those most important life-long acquired documents integrated into enclosures in one binder. The Author can not express strong enough the need for every person to order a copy for their own individual use.

The print was selected for easy reading and kind to the eye sight. The language used in this guide is meant to be informal. The Abbreviation **GFMS** identifies the title, **Guide For My Survivor**, and is used throughout this guide for reducing space.

For the purpose of this guide, the use of the word <u>ANNUITANT</u> used throughout this guide, means people working for salary, wages, self employed, in receipt of retirement annuity or by other means of income but, income is not always a prerequisite. The word <u>SURVIVOR</u>, are; spouse, (widow or widower), family member or elected beneficiary.

The Guide For My Survivor upon completion, will become a sensitive document and will be one of annuitant's most important personal investments in his or her life time. Family members or friends should encourage and help annuitant to correlate (put together) this document to the fullest extent. It is strongly recommended couples work together in completing their own GFMS

Why should annuitants purchase the Guide For My Survivor? For many reasons;
   * To establish comfort (ease of mind) and financial security to the fullest extent possible for spouse, family or friend.
   * To insure survivor has all documentation in order to settle estate of annuitant with minimum effort and difficulty.
   * To insure annuitants (after demise) receive their final wish as they instructed in their guide for my survivor.
   * To instill in children's minds that annuitant is responsible and cares for their health and well being and that he or she loves them very much.
   * To encourage spouse, children, family and friends the importance of preparing a GFMS for their own personal need.
   * That each annuitant purchase their own GFMS. What one person wishes may not apply to the other. To file their "own" personal documents.
   * That each annuitant's hard earned benefits are different than his or her spouse or family members.
   * That the chances of annuitant and spouse dying together in an accident are greater in today's transportation environment than ever before, not excluding fatal accidents at work, at home, on the farm and from natural disasters.
   * That today's world instability, conflicts and wars are spreading, threatening and causing casualties in our armed forces and civilian citizens throughout the world. Imagine the difficulties the survivors of casualties in the September 11,2001 catastrophes are going through to settle their loved ones estates. Let us prepare now. Order a copy of GFMS for all members of your family and inform other relatives and friends of the importance of having an organized file for their survivor.

The advancement of medicines in Western Countries now provide people of all ages the opportunity to live longer and healthier lives. Unfortunately, some people just keep procrastinating (putting off) their responsibility of preparing and consolidating their most important documentation procured throughout their lives. With the help of this guide, there is no need to wait. Simply follow the procedures identified in the contents, text and enclosures.

When an annuitant, family member or friend passes away, they leave behind survivor or family members scrambling to search for those necessary documents needed to settle their loved one's estate. The GFMS is the best and most direct method to complete settlement of an estate in minimum time.

Often, during and after the grieving, the survivor continues with the burden of searching for lost or misfiled documentation. Many families have gone on living without claiming insurance or other benefits because they could not find them. How many times have you heard or read about the family life insurance policy that was purchased, then later dropped or discontinued because of missed payments. How the decedent failed to mention to his or her spouse that their life insurance had lapsed or discontinued. Numerous survivors have lost monetary benefits because they just simply didn't follow-up on active disability claims which the decedent had ongoing while still alive. Survivors have a right to follow-up on open file disability claims. Claims by the survivor concerning the decedent is based on evidence submitted and the cause of death. Final approval or disapproval rests on the decision by the governing authority. Many survivors are awakened back to reality. What happened? How could he or she let this happen, and so on. These are questions many of us have experienced. **I want my family to know that my personal affairs and documentation are in order, "before my demise".**

AUTHOR'S REFLECTION

MY PAST EXPERIENCE AND KNOWLEDGE CONCERNING ESTATE SETTLEMENTS , ASSISTING FRIENDS AND OTHER PEOPLE PREPARED ME FOR WRITING THIS GUIDE TO HELP SURVIVORS IN TIME OF NEED. I THEREFORE ENCOURAGE EVERYBODY TO PURCHASE THIS GUIDE AND TO REACH DEEP IN YOUR SOUL AND BRING OUT THAT COURAGE TO COMPLETE YOUR PERSONAL AFFAIRS FOR THE WELL-BEING AND FUTURE OF YOUR LOVED ONES. INSTILL IN YOUR THOUGHTS A POSITIVE COMMITMENT TO TAKE ACTION IN WRITTEN FORM SO YOUR SURVIVOR OR BENEFICIARY WILL NOT ENCOUNTER PROBLEMS AFTER YOU ARE GONE.. GOD BLESS US ALL.

PREFACE

The idea of writing a guide for my wife and family, focused my attention immediately after the September 11, 2001 tragedy with the terrorist attacks on United States of America, New York Twin Towers and the Pentagon. I proclaim that it is very important that my wife, family and all peoples should not have to encounter enormous expense and difficulties when claiming their survivor financial benefits when the time comes to settle their loved one's estate.

These heinous attacks which caused unexpected tragic death to our citizens and friends, leaving thousands of survivors and family suffering, mourning and in desolation, inspired me to write this guide I titled: Guide For My Survivor--GFMS.

This guide was initially intended only for my wife and family. As my writing progressed and the style and form began to take shape, I decided to format it into separate enclosures with separate titles to accommodate supporting documents. This prompted me to offer it to the general public. Why? Because in many months of my research for similar books or guides, I found not one that literally presents a thorough and easy to follow guide on how to correlate and maintain a complete personal file in a two or three-inch binder.

The tragedy and loss of thousands of lives in such a short span of hours re-ignited my anguish, mental pain and suffering experienced with the loss of my own mother and father, family members and friends. I have first hand experience with settling my parent's estate and helping survivors of friends who have passed away. I have experience in military escort duties of deceased military to their final resting place. I saw many people experience problems in locating their loved one's (decedent's) personal documents to settle the estate. For many years, I helped and advised survivors in claiming survivor benefits which otherwise may not have known about what, where and how to file claims. The main objective here, is to prepare all your personal affairs and put documentation in order, that is the purpose of the Guide For My Survivor.

DEDICATION

This guide is dedicated in memory of my Mother, Maria Emerenciana Gonzales Pineda, my Father, Torribio Pineda and family members who have passed away, I miss them dearly. In memory of all the lives lost in the September 11, 2001 terrorist attacks and to our military and civilian citizens and all other nations citizens who have lost their life in the war against terrorism around the world.

TEXT

© 2002

HOW TO ASSEMBLE GUIDE INTO AN ORDERLY DOCUMENT:

The annuitant must first perform the following to make this Guide For My Survivor, GFMS into a functioning document. Include your spouse, children or friend in the assembly process. As a result, they will learn and with your permission may help you complete your GFMS.

1. Before removing the cover or any pages from the bound paperback guide, take the time to read and familiarize yourself with the remainder of the GFMS to understand all the information and documentation needed.

2. Place the binder in front of you and ready the binder with prongs open and insert all the empty sheet protectors into the right side of the binder. Next, cut-off cover and pages in sequence and place in document protectors. Now place it into the left-side of the three hole prongs of binder as you turn a page. Follow the sequence until you have completed the entire GFMS. Close the three-hole prongs and turn the entire GFMS to the right-side of binder. Next, TAB the enclosures 1 through 12 for easy reference. Place the <u>TAB over the document protector</u>, not the paper.

3. Use a pen for all permanent data (information) and a Nr. 2 pencil for all data subject to change. Before filling in data in the blank lists at enclosures, make extra copies as recommended or as needed, then write-in clearly or print as much data as possible. Keep the extra copies in same document protector for use when needed. Permission for reproduction is granted only for those lists and letters indicated at enclosures. Upon completing as much as possible, return here to next step, item number four.

4. At your discretion find a witness, other than your beneficiary, then sign and date the signature block at end of text, page 16. The witness' signature is only to authenticate the annuitant's signature and not to verify information or completion of guide.

5. Prepare a binder or file label and place it on your binder for easy identification. Print your label in **BOLD LETTERS** if possible.

6. At this stage, go to enclosure Nr. One. If you already have a LAST WILL AND TESTAMENT, insert it into the sheet protector and place it in binder directly behind enclosure Nr. One.

11

Do NOT take the WILL apart or write-in notes or changes because doing so will invalidate your WILL.

If you do not have a WILL, make yourself a reminder on a stick-on note to seek advice from your attorney on last wills and testament. Attach the sticky-note to enclosure Nr. One, until you complete the action. Continue on to enclosure Nr. Two, fill in the information. Follow through with the remainder of the enclosures until all documentation has been added and information is entered. Your spouse, family member or friend can be of big help, so seek their help and in turn you can help them with their GFMS.

7. Inform your spouse, executor, family member or friend where the binder, labeled; Guide For My Survivor, is kept or secured. While working on your GFMS and especially after completion, it becomes personal, sensitive and confidential in nature. Remember to secure you GFMS when you are not reviewing or working on it.

SECURITY AND SAFE KEEPING OF DOCUMENTS:

The subject about how or where to secure your documents and valuables is a long standing contradiction and disagreement. If you put them in a bank safe deposit box, your survivor may not be able to get access soon after your death.

If you keep them in a file cabinet or box at home, they may get misplaced or even lost. If you keep them in a personal safe under combination or lock and key, where do you secure your safe? Where do you secure your key? Who must be informed where the key or combination is kept?

Obviously, there are a lot of factors to consider; your financial status, do you own or rent a home, do you have a permanent residence or do you move periodically like construction workers, military personnel, civil service personnel and their families?

So what should you do? If you are a financially secure individual, you can afford a bank safe deposit box or a fireproof safe at home. If you are a retiree or pensioner living on a budget, at a minimum use a metal filing cabinet with lock and key. Caution; secure your safe and filing cabinet away from potential flooding areas like basements or ground level floors in homes near potential flood grounds and rivers. Do not keep expensive jewelry, cameras and such items in the same file cabinet with your GFMS and other important papers, secure them separately. However, people with heavy, spacious, and anchored fire-proof safes can combine all their valuables and important documents together.. Insure your spouse and executor know where your GFMS is located.

If you keep your GFMS in a private safe or file cabinet, insure you separate it from other files. Again, inform your spouse, executor, friend or beneficiary on how he or she can obtain access, with key, safe combination or both.

INFORMATION FOR ANNUITANT:

This guide is prepared to ease the burden of the survivor's worries to maximum intent. If you, do not have a <u>Last Will and Testament and a Revocable Living Trust, I</u> strongly recommend having both to save probate and some legal fees.

Again I remind you, when you fill-in your personal information, fill in all applicable blanks In pencil where information is subject to change, ie; temporary address and telephone numbers as they occur.

Write in N/A, meaning <u>Not Applicable,</u> in the blank spaces if it does not apply to you. Do not leave spaces or questions unanswered. Be considerate of your survivor and or your executor.

Telephone referrals of local, state or government agencies are listed in this guide to a very minimum because, they would be too many to list. It is best for you to look-up local and national telephone numbers needed and list them in the appropriate blanks and enclosures for survivor or executor to use.

The loss of a family member or friend affects all family immediately at the loss of their loved one, followed by extended periods of grief after their loss. Normally, the spouse and close family members are devastated and struggle on how to handle the annuitant's estate. Don't let this happen to your survivor.

It is a good policy NOT to release original documentation. Make copies (such as certificates of birth and marriage) and have the copies certified by a public notary and send only the certified copy. For copies of divorce decree, you must order them as "court certified copies" from the jurisdiction where the divorce took place, there is a fee so call ahead and find out before ordering. Information at enclosures will guide you on what documents and how many you need to have notarized.

HOW CAN YOU HELP YOUR SPOUSE, FAMILY OR FRIEND?

Purchasing and completing the Guide For My Survivor by annuitants can eliminate survivor's difficulties by ninety-five percent for the majority of people. The other five percent are variables, such as missing pieces of information needed to complete an action. Survivor must follow-up on claims pending, like disability or worker compensation awaiting action or decision that were submitted prior to annuitant's death.

These missing pieces are all potential benefits to the survivor when they take action to follow-up and complete claims. A completed GFMS will enhance benefit potential and expedite claims. For more details, see enclosure-four where pending actions may apply.

Annuitants can help by not waiting to fill in the blanks in the text of this guide and attach to enclosures, the documentation needed to settle their estates. This guide is self explanatory and easy to follow in sequence of information.

Most important, don't leave your loved ones in the dark. Discuss this guide with your elected beneficiary (spouse, family member or, a friend if no family members remain).

Work together to complete this guide so your spouse and or elected executor are completely familiar with guide, contents and where filed or stored.

Other guides or checklists mention some, part of, or all the requirements needed but, do not mention how to carefully organize a centralized file document with all the information needed as does the guide for my survivor. Take advantage.

Your GFMS is carefully designed to provide the information needed to efficiently settle an estate of majority of annuitants. Once filled-in and documents are attached as enclosures, this guide then becomes a very effective document

Some estates of wealthy persons and with enormous assets are best handled by lawyers, legal accounting and other professional services. However, wealthy or not it is strongly encouraged that this guide be obtained and used by all annuitants as a basis for well organized documentation.

You as the annuitant can honestly help your family and friends by telling them about the essence of purchasing a copy of the GFMS for their own use. In addition, you can do a great favor for your children by gifting a copy of the GFMS for their own personal record keeping. Start by adding their birth and educational certificates and other important records as they grow-up. You may even add individual yearly school photos and a copy of their first and follow-up renewals of their drivers license. Show them and teach them throughout their school years the importance of keeping their GFMS in a current and orderly manner. When they become adults and eventually get married, they will have learned the importance and responsibility of keeping up their GFMS. Encourage your children, family members, relatives and friends to purchase a GFMS for their spouse, children and their future generations. Purchase a copy of the GFMS for your spouse and each of your children. It is one investment you will never regret.

14

Your spouse needs his or her own GFMS, especially if employed there is a need for track of employment, retirement data in later years and special wishes in case she or he precedes you in death.

PERSONAL INFORMATION:

This section of text contains information pertaining only to you, the annuitant. The blank spaces must be filled in to fullest extent. It is at the enclosures where you add data and the supporting documents pertaining to you and your family to complete the GFMS. At the enclosures are more detail information on what and how to add or secure the documents.

Name:_____.
          (First)   (Middle)   (Last)

Date and Place of Birth: _____.
           (Month, day, year)   (Town)   (State)

Social Security Number:_____ U.S. Citizenship: Yes_____ No _____.

Other Citizenship:_____ Alien Registered:_____.
        (Country)   (Registration Nr.) (Month, Day, Year)

Naturalized Citizen? _____.
    (Naturalization Nr.)   (Month, day, Year)   (Place of naturalization)

Current U.S. Address: _____

_____.

Permanent Address:_____
      (Home of Record - Where you were born, give Town, County and State name)

_____.

Military Address:_____
            (United states, APO, FPO, etc.)

_____.

Foreign Address: _____
       (Complete, economy residential address where living oversea)

_____.

Write-in the following contact information where you are <u>currently</u> residing:

Home telephone # _____ Work telephone # _____.
E-mail Address: _____ Fax Number: _____.

Are you signed up to be an ORGAN DONOR? Yes___ No____. If Yes, Where? _____

_____
   (Family Doctor ____? Hospital____? Driver license ____? (Give address and telephone Number)

Do you have an attorney? Yes ___ No ___. _____
                                                      (Attorney's Telephone Number)

_____
   (First Name)   (Last Name)   (Address)

_____

Describe your present health condition; Excellent ___, Good ___, Fair ___, Poor ____ or
Bad ____? If other than excellent or good, what caused your health conditions? :

_____

_____

_____

_____

Are you partly disabled? - 10% ____, 30% ____, Other ____%, or Fully Disabled - 100%
percent____? See enclosure -four for details if applicable.

Do you have Disability Applications pending for approval? Yes ___ No ___. If yes, see
enclosure-four for additional details and enclosure-ten for location of medical files and
copy of disability claim.

This concludes all the information needed in this text. To continue would only be
duplicating what is already written in the enclosures. The table of contents will refer you
to enclosures where you are seeking the information by subject.

_____Date: _____
Annuitant's Signature (sign and date with ink pen)

_____
Annuitant's Full Name (please print)

_____Date: _____
Witness' Signature (sign and date with ink pen)

_____
Witness' Full Name (please print) / Witness' Address

ENCLOSURE - ONE

© 2002

SUBJECT: Wills, Testaments and Trusts.

1. PURPOSE: a. To determine why and the need to prepare a <u>last will and testament</u>. b. To decide if you wish to have a <u>living will.</u> c. To decide if and when you may need a <u>durable power of attorney</u> for HEALTH CARE. d. To determine the absolute need to establish a <u>revocable living trust or a bypass trust.</u> e. To inform the survivor and executor on the usage and function of annuitant's death certificate.

2. LAST WILL AND TESTAMENT: A will is a written document or instrument which the annuitant (person who makes the will) states his or her wishes in handling and distribution of property upon his or her death.

When you get your Will, insert it in it's entirety in a document protector and place it at this enclosure. "Do not take your Will apart". If Will does not fit protector, split only the right side (not the bottom) of protector with a knife or scissors. Insert the Will into protector and staple protector to document only at the top side to secure it in place.

3. DO YOU NEED A WILL?: A Last Will And Testament and a Revocable Living Trust (**RLT**) are strongly recommended for estate settlement of your physical and monetary assets. See an attorney in the state which you reside or claim as a home of record. If you're in the military, civil service or military retiree, see a Judge Advocate Legal Representative at the military base nearest you. State laws concerning Wills may vary from state to state when governing the execution of a Will and administration of annuitant's estate. If you have a large estate and investments, you should have a well prepared Will, a RLT and you should have a preferred attorney named to advise the executor or survivor on settling your estate. What if both you and your spouse both died in an accident? Wouldn't you prefer to have a will and RLT to settle your estate? With a Will and RLT you would be assured your estate would be distributed as you would wish and without family conflict.

In the Will, the annuitant names an executor to handle or carry out its instructions. Usually the annuitant names a spouse, family member or friend as executor.

The person named as executor must file the Will In the court and follow its instructions under the supervision of a probate court. The RLT must also be presented to the court so the monetary assets administered by the RLT are not entered in probate court. See your attorney for details.

If you do not leave a Will, your estate property will be distributed in accordance with the laws of your state.

Other valuable and very important questions you should ask an attorney are about your concern if you should have a <u>Living Will, Durable Powers of Attorney</u> and <u>Revocable Living Trust:</u>

4. LIVING WILL: A living will provides instructions about what should be done when someone is terminally ill and unable to make or communicate a decision concerning medical treatment.

5. DURABLE POWER OF ATTORNEY FOR HEALTH CARE: This is an important legal document. Before executing this document you should know the facts and power this document gives the person you designate as your agent (The Attorney-in-Fact). This document gives the power to your agent to make health care decisions for you when you no longer capable of making health care decisions for yourself. As other legal documents, always contact your legal advisor or attorney-for facts, advise and preparation.

6. REVOCABLE LIVING TRUST: A revocable living trust is legal under which an annuitant transfers financial assets to a named trust. Monies transferred into the trust remain the property of the grantor (annuitant) as long as the grantor remains alive. The annuitant can decide at any time that the standby trustee named in the trust document, can begin managing the trust's assets. This trustee can be a family member or preferably a professional bank's trust officer to assume management of the financial trust. Money earned by the trust assets become part of the annuitant's annual income and must be reported in income tax filing. **Why mention trusts under wills?** A trust significantly reduces estate processing costs and minimizes delays in distribution of financial assets to survivor or beneficiaries. An annuitant needs a WILL for the purpose of disposing annuitant's personal belongings and assets not transferred to the trust while the annuitant was alive.

7. DO YOU NEED A REVOCABLE LIVING TRUST?: If you don't have a revocable living trust, I strongly recommend you seek advice from your banking facility adviser and learn of the advantages. In summary, a revocable living trust is a document stating who controls your assets while you are alive and what will happen to them when you have passed away.

When you die, the trust passes your assets <u>without court or probate fees</u> directly to your survivor or beneficiary as you direct. Regardless of how little money you make or how wealthy you are, it is worth having for the sake of your family or beneficiary. This does not mean you should not have a WILL , because having both is to you and your survivor's advantage while you are alive and after your gone.

18

Discuss this with your attorney and bank officer. Check with your Investments Representative at your bank, some banks or credit unions offer free processing and no fee for opening a RLT through them. All accounts with your name on them including all assets with a title on them, "except retirement accounts" can or should be transferred into the name of the RLT.

8. BYPASS TRUST: If you are one of the fortunate people to be wealthy and there are many, I strongly recommend and encourage you to see a lawyer without any delay.

9. CERTIFICATE OF DEATH: Annuitant's Certificate of Death will be issued to or obtained by the survivor or executor of estate at the time of annuitant's demise.

Upon receipt and for record purpose, immediately file one original death certificate at this enclosure. Use the second original to make certified copies. The number of copies needed varies from family to family. On the average, ten (10) to fifteen (15) certified copies should suffice, depending on your assets.

In some cases when claiming a life insurance for payment, the survivor may be asked to furnish an original certificate of death. Although this is no longer a common place or practice, it is advisable to obtain two original certificates of death from hospital or doctor who certified the death of the deceased.

Should a life insurance company or government agency request an <u>original</u> certificate, ask them if they mean a <u>certified</u> copy verses an <u>original.</u> Normally, a certified copy should be sufficient.

If you have a favorite attorney you wish to handle or assist in settlement of your estate, write his name, address, telephone number here and any other information essential to your survivor:

_____
_____
_____
_____
_____

Write your elected executor's name, address and telephone number here;

_____
_____
_____
_____
_____

NOTES FOR YOUR SPOUSE OR EXECUTOR

ENCLOSURE - TWO

© 2002

SUBJECT: Family and Friends Notification List.

1. PURPOSE: a. To have a ready list of family and friends to be notified immediately after the annuitant's death. b. To reduce the burden on the grieving survivor from having to lookup or locate addresses and telephone numbers of family and friends. c. To expedite notice to family members away from home in the military, civil service or contract service.

2. NOTIFICATION LIST: Annuitant should write-in the immediate family members (mother, father, brothers and sisters), followed by aunts, uncles, nephews etc, then friends and colleagues. Use a PENCIL for filling in address and telephone number since they are subject to change.

To be effective, the list must be complete, with full name, address and telephone number. When annuitant is fully satisfied with list, Xerox one (1) copy, and mark it as a copy and attach at this enclosure behind the original list. The copy is recommended for survivor or executor to take to the Red Cross along <u>with a certified or original death certificate</u>. The representative at the   Red Cross will inform survivor who they can notify from the list. The remaining members on the list can be notified by survivor, executor or a friend via telephone, telegram, fax, e-mail, or to distant friends, by postal mail.

3. AMERICAN RED CROSS: When the annuitant passes away, survivor and executor can and should use the AMERICAN RED CROSS for notifying family members of the deceased, serving in the MILITARY, CIVIL SERVICE or GOVERNMENT CONTRACT WORK overseas or away from home. Military and civil service member's organizations need official verification of death of a family member in order to grant emergency leave from his or her place of work or assignment.

Write-in, the nearest Red Cross address and telephone number for use by survivor:
Address: _____

_____

Telephone number: _____

4. NOTIFICATION BY MAIL: If annuitant so desires, he or she my want certain members on the list to be notified only by letter. List them last and annotate with a dividing note: "Notify following persons of my demise, only by letter mail." These persons may be long standing friends or colleagues living long distances away. Survivor can perform this special request after all other priorities and as time becomes available.

5. NAME AND ADDRESS LIST: Before filling-in, use the blank form, page 23 or 24 to reproduce extra blank pages if needed.

Family and Friends Notification List. Date prepared or updated: _____

FULL NAME	COMPLETE ADDRESS	A/C	TELE Nr.

FULL NAME	COMPLETE ADDRESS	A/C	TELE Nr.

23

FULL NAME	COMPLETE ADDRESS	A/C	TELE Nr.

24

ENCLOSURE - THREE

© 2002

SUBJECT: Funeral and Burial Arrangements:

1. PURPOSE: a. To help annuitant prepare for the inevitable before his or her demise. b. To prepare spouse and family with the fact that all documentation is in order to settle funeral , burial and estate settlement. c. To feel comfortable with your family and them knowing that you truly care and love them.

2. LIFE IN GENERAL: It is rather easy to go through life getting an education, that is, until you have to work for a living. Going to work to establish a career and then into retirement is a difficult task, even more so being married, raising a family and educating them. But what is life all about if it is not for finding the right partner for purpose of making a comfortable home and then raising a family. Life has it's ups and downs but, with serious commitments and dedication, a couples' lives can be very rewarding.

People go through life thinking about dying, but instead of discussing it with their family about what happens after they die, they block it out of their mind. They avoid the subject not realizing the impact it will have on their survivor and family. I have heard many times from people that they do not have the time or they are too busy to organize their personal papers. Life can end any moment and when we least expect it, may it be through illness or accident. We must, out of self-respect and respect for our family, carefully prepare for our demise as early as possible. I strongly encourage you to make your preferences crystal clear to your spouse and family what you wish to have done with your remains. Having your personal affairs ready, documents in order and details worked out will certainly curtail some heartfelt pain and provide relief to your spouse and family.

You worked all your life to take care of your family while you are alive, so why not initiate a plan of action for your funeral like you have for their health and financial well being for when you are gone. You need to share your wishes for funeral arrangement with your loved ones. There is no better time to start that process than now.

3. SEEKING HELP: If you are in military service or government service, you should ask your commander or personnel office for assistance in locating the nearest survivor assistance office. The office that will assist your surviving spouse may be identified as; retirement services office, survivor assistance office, personal affairs office or casualty assistance office. Some offices may appoint a survivor assistance officer to help take care of most arrangements and benefits.

25

Military personnel and retirees, contact the nearest military base for assistance. Find out where the office is located and write it in the following space:

* _____

(Installation where office is located)   (Name of assistance office)

* _____

(Building Number)   (Telephone Number)

Active military personnel: * "Keep this information up to date when you change bases." If you are TDY or unaccompanied tour, leave your GFMS <u>with your spouse</u> in a secure location. <u>If you are single</u> and you have your GFMS completed, enter a notice in your official personnel file located at your personnel office. Insure your notice states where your GFMS is located, ie, foot locker, wall locker etc. Second option is to send it to your next of kin or elected executor. Review your GFMS each time you go home on leave for updating and accuracy.

4. FUNERAL AND BURIAL: The following information is a suggested guide format for providing needed information for your survivor concerning your funeral arrangements. If you wish to add more information to the subject, please do so in paragraph 5. Special Requests Or Instructions:

    a.. **RELIGION OR DENOMINATION;** _____ Your Clergyman:

_____

(List name, address and telephone number of Clergyman)

Obituary and Eulogy; If you, wish to write a special announcement for the obituary or even prepare a narration relating to your life, by all means do so in paragraph 5. You have already helped your survivor with the obituary by listing your family and relatives at enclosure - two It would be very helpful if in your own words, prepare a biographical writing for your survivor to use. Attach a <u>good quality photo of you (2"x2")</u> of your choice to include in your story. An outline of special occations and accomplishments with dates or age of occurrence would help if you wish to keep your writing short.

    b. **RECOMMENDED HELP;** List names, addresses and telephone numbers of family members, friends or associates who you recommend to be of help to your survivor:

Name	Address	Telephone Number

c. **MEMBERSHIP IN PRIVATE ASSOCIATIONS;** If you are a member of an association that might be helpful to your spouse or survivor, suggest that you list them and indicate what assistance your survivor may expect. Such organizations can be; Veteran of Foreign Wars, American Legion or State Veterans Department nearest your place of residence:

Name	Address	Telephone Number

d. **BURIAL PLOT;** Have you pre-purchased a burial plot? What is the name of cemetery and where is it located? If yes, attach original or copy of purchase to this enclosure. Indicate status or plan here: _____

_____

_____

_____

e. **FUNERAL HOME;** List your funeral home preference and if known, the name, address and telephone number of the funeral director. It is a good idea to find current cost of mandatory procedures by the funeral home for arrangements and burial. Ask the director how and where he can cut costs for your funeral expenses. Have your spouse or executor accompany you, when you visit the funeral home director. If your not happy with his or answers, check with other funeral homes for comparison. A careful choice is in order ahead of time, with respect to funeral expenses. Naturally, expenses go up on a yearly basis, so if you stay healthy visit your funeral director every two or three years. Name the funeral home you have selected here:

(Name of Director)	(Hours he can be reached)	(Telephone Number)

(Name of Funeral Home)	(Address)	(Telephone Number)

f. **THINKING ABOUT BEING CREMATED?** If you desire to be cremated, ask your funeral director for instructions. Ask about State law requirements. List your findings and decision about cremation under special instructions. Don't be shy to ask about cost savings.

g. **YOUR CHURCH AND CLERGYMAN;** With respect to your religious preference or affiliation, your survivor may want to request the assistance of your clergyman before beginning funeral arrangements. See paragraph 4a above.

27

h. **MILITARY VETERANS;** If you are veteran of military service or of foreign war, do you want to be buried in national cemetery? If yes, where? Have prior arrangements been made? What VA Center must survivor or executor contact? List information here:

(Name of VA Center)	(Address)	(Telephone Number)

If you want to be buried in a national cemetery, write in the information to expedite request and verification:

(Rank & Grade at Discharge or Retirement)	(Military Service Branch)	(Date of Last Active Duty)

(Date of Birth)	(Social Security Number)	(Military Service Nr.)

(Type Discharge	(Type Retirement: Disability, Reserve)

i. **UNIFORM, HONOR GUARD, MEMORIAL SERVICE;** Do you as a veteran prefer burial in uniform?, Military Honor Guard?, Memorial service? If yes to any of these questions, do you have a uniform with awards and decorations already pinned and ready. If not, ready your uniform and store it where your spouse or survivor can find it. Your answer here: _____

_____
_____
_____
_____

j. **OTHER BENEFITS;** VA headstone? VA expense assistance for burial plot and burial expense, do you qualify? Call and ask your nearest VA Center or contact the nearest VA Regional Office by dialing 1-800-872-1000. Write results of your call here: _____

_____
_____
_____
_____

k. **SOCIAL SECURITY BENEFITS;** Social Security will also pay a lump-sum death benefit to the surviving spouse or eligible child of person who died and was fully or currently insured. The maximum payable is $255. Social Security Survivor Benefits can be applied for by calling 1-800-772-1213. It is very important that you and your spouse become familiar with Social Security survivor benefits and that your local office is contacted as soon as possible after death occurs. Most of these claims can be claimed and handled by telephone to expedite benefits.

Contact your local office and write down their address and telephone number here:

_____
(Local Social Security Office - Complete Address and Telephone Number)

    l. **PALLBEARERS;** If you desire, list your pallbearers and where to contact them:

_____
   (Name)   (Address)   (Telephone Number)

_____

_____

_____

_____

    m. **FLOWERS;** Do you want flowers? (or in place of flowers): _____
_____
_____
_____
_____

    n. **MEMORIALS;** Memorials and recognition. Enter under SPECIAL REQUEST or INSTRUCTIONS.

    o. **IN CASE BOTH PARENTS DIE TOGETHER IN AN ACCIDENT;** Should my spouse and I, both die together in an accident, a key family member designated as our executor will be notified by the police or designated officials. Always carry an EMERGENCY NOTIFICATION CARD in your wallet, your automobile registration folder and passport if in a foreign country. Our executor will know where to locate our Guide For My Survivor - GFMS. Our Last Will and Testament and/or Living Trust is, with other necessary information also in our GFMS to settle our estates.

5. SPECIAL REQUESTS or INSTRUCTIONS: Use the following lined spaces, to write special requests and instructions. Personal effects: Enter here what you want done (disposition) with your special or personal effects not otherwise legally specified in your last will and testament or living trust. I.E.; Hobby hand tools, belt buckles, miniature houses, etc. Use white lined tablet paper if additional space is needed. _____

_____

_____

ENCLOSURE - FOUR

© 2002

SUBJECT: Reporting Annuitant's Death.

1. PURPOSE: a. To prepare survivor on what to do with annuitant's pay soon as possible after annuitant's demise. b. To inform survivor with latest information concerning annuitant's employment and retirement status for claiming eligible survivor benefits. d. To inform survivor about annuitant's pending approval/disapproval of disability application (if applicable). e. To keep current record of employment and retirement on data sheets. f. To supply survivor with sample letters for reporting death of annuitant.

2. GENERAL: Annuitant must pay special attention when writing down and attaching supporting documents. Addresses and telephone numbers must be listed correctly in the employment and retirement data sheets for survivor's immediate use. The financial claims and settlements are survivor and executor's highest priority to accomplish with due respect to annuitant's death.

3. ANNUIITANT'S PAY STOPS: Annuitant's entitlement to retirement pay **stops** on the date of his or her death. The surviving spouse (or other survivors) and the annuitant's bank have no authority to cash any government checks made payable to annuitant. Should either receive a social security, military or civil service retirement paycheck or an electronic fund transfer payable to the annuitant, those un-cashed checks or funds for that entire month must be returned to the retirement pay section of that agency stating the reason. When returning an un-cashed check, it is "advisable" to send it back to the agency CERTIFIED with RETURN RECEIPT REQUESTED form.

In most all cases, someone is entitled to an adjusted portion of annuitant's retirement pay at the time of his or her death. In order for the survivor to be qualified or eligible to receive retirement or annuity benefits, the survivor or executor must report as soon as possible the annuitant's death to agencies listed in attached data sheets, institutions and agency list. The reporting of annuitant's death will activate any survivor benefits he or she may have coming from listed agencies if eligible survivor annuity benefits exist. The reporting of annuitant's death is of highest of priority because, it involves adjustment and transaction of survivor's annuity. This is where having an elected executor and a complete and well kept up to date GFMS is so important.

4. EMPLOYMENT AND RETIREMENT AGENCIES: The list of retirement or annuity benefits agencies can be very long and for that reason, only the most common agencies are listed here. If the annuitant does not see his or her agency or firm listed, then by all means name the firm or agency under other employment benefits, i.e.; Current Employment, other retirement agency, Trust Funds, IRA - Individual Retirement Account, TSP Thrift Savings Plan, 401(k) plans and many other employer sponsored plans. Follow-up by filling in a data sheet concerning your employment, retirement agency or other potential annuity income.

The most common annuity or retirement benefit agencies are listed below. You my want to list the telephone numbers in the blank spaces below for the convenience of your survivor if they apply to you. Otherwise, they will be listed in your employment or retirement data sheet.

--------Social Security Benefits, toll free telephone number: 1-800-772-1213

--------Federal Civil Service Benefits, to report the death of an annuitant or survivor, call The Office of Personnel Management, Retirement Information Office at 1-202-606-0500 (TDD 1-202-606-0511).

--------State Civil Service Benefits List the State Civil Service Office telephone for reporting death of annuitant or survivor here; _____

--------Military Service Benefits. For reporting the death of Army, Navy, Marine Corps, Air Force retiree annuitant or survivor, call 1-800-269-5170. To request a form , required for sending the Death Certificate, call this number 1-216-522-6680.

--------Veteran/s Administration (VA) Benefits. (List the telephone number of your nearest VA Office in your State, here; _____

--------Railroad Employment Benefits. (List the telephone number of your railroad agency finance office, here; _____

--------Self Employment Benefits. (List annuitant's business office telephone here;

_____

--------Approved Disability Benefits. These could fall under any of above benefits if annuitant became disabled while performing work related activities. List telephone number of agency if not listed above; _____
If annuitant is receiving disability retirement, record the information in the retirement data sheet in pages 39 and 40.

--------Other Employment Agencies for Benefits. Record and annotate your current job or employment agency in the Employment Data Sheet, pages 37 and 38 for the record. Make one or more blank copies for future employment record.

5. PENDING APPROVAL/DISAPPROVAL OF DISABILITY APPLICATION: If annuitant has a disability application pending and he or she dies, <u>it's important that the survivor notify the agency</u> and follow-up on the claim. It could be that annuitant's death was work related and <u>could qualify survivor for annuity benefits</u>. (List the agency telephone number of pending disability application, here; _____
The agency will ask survivor for a certified copy of death certificate and probably additional or most recent medical proof.

Due to the usually large volume of disability claims, insure a complete copy of the original claim is filed in a safe location. Place only a <u>copy</u> of the letter forwarding the claim packet at this enclosure. Write a Memorandum For Record - MFR, what actions were or are being taken to follow-up on claim. If telephone inquiries were made, prepare a detail MFR of the conversation and file a copy here. All original inquiries or actions after submission of claim must be filed with packet. Also, write down in enclosure Nr. 10, where claim packet is filed. **Never submit original medical documents,** only copies are required since they will not be returned to you. When you write a letter forwarding additional medical evidence, always insure you send the one with original signature to avoid delays or non-acceptance. Keep original medical evidence submitted neatly attached to the copy of forwarding letter and record its location at enclosure - ten of this guide.

Should the annuitant die of illness, pre-existing, service connected, on the job injury or health hazard, such proof can be submitted by survivor as follow-up to original claim but, now the burden of proof rests on the survivor of the deceased. Survivor or beneficiary may then qualify for annuity due to annuitant's disability even after annuitant's demise. ONLY THE AGENCY to which the annuitant made claim can determine if there is qualifying compensation for the survivor based on evidence submitted in writing, presented in person or both.

Agencies with receipt of most claims for disability, compensation or other benefits, to name a few are; Social Security, Veteran's Administration, Office of Personnel Management - OPM (includes most federal agencies), State Agencies and Business Corporations. Annuitants filing claims for disability compensation and other benefits must wait months or up to three-years for a final decision. <u>Most claims require filing appeals with limited response time, so be prepared.</u> Annuitants and survivors should have patience and follow-up periodically through their local agencies such as; state or regional social security office, nearest VA claims center or a lawyer helping with claim. Usually, a local claims representative is assigned to handle the claim when request for assistance is made.

These representatives can open doors with direct access where annuitant or survivor cannot get answers without encountering delays and difficulty, not to mention the high telephone cost of waiting for an answer while they put you on hold.

6. EMPLOYMENT AND RETIREMENT DATA SHEETS: Pages 37 - 40, to this enclosure are employment and retirement data sheets you can use to record address, telephone numbers and other information that apply to you, the annuitant. Keep your data sheets up to date by reviewing your GFMS every three months or as changes occur.

Make three (3) copies of the employment data sheet and two (2) copies of the retirement data sheet. Always keep one blank copy of each to Xerox additional copies if needed. Use document protectors for inserting the data sheets and all supporting documents.

Examples of supporting documents are: salary, wage, retiree and annuity pay statements. Certificates, letters, orders of employment and retirement.

7. SAMPLE NOTIFICATION LETTERS FOR REPORTING DEATH: The sample letters, pages 41 - 44 are for use by either annuitant, spouse, remaining survivor or executor. The first sample is regarding the death of annuitant and the second sample is regarding the death of annuitant's spouse. Should both annuitant and spouse die in an accident or catastrophe, survivor or executor can modify the letter of notification since both deaths would have to be reported to whom it may concern. This is the main reason for keeping the data sheets, institution and agency list current as mentioned in paragraph 3, above.

8. INSTITUTIONS AND AGENCY NOTIFICATION LIST: Strongly recommend annuitant write-in all the institutions and agencies where business is actively conducted. The list of INSTITUTIONS are; banks, insurance companies, credit unions, loan companies, etc. AGENCIES are; retirement services, such as corporations, trust funds or private investments, government services like social security, office of personnel management, veteran's administration or armed forces finances for military retirees. This list will save the survivor or executor much time and effort.

Most institutions and agencies, once notified by telephone, may request a certified copy of death certificate and other information if needed. The survivor or executor can then annotate date and time agency was notified, information requested by agency and date action was completed. Which ever the procedure requested by the agency or institution, follow-up soon as possible to eliminate delays.

INSTITUTION AND AGENCY NOTIFICATION LIST

* For Annuitant, ** For Survivor. For extra copies of list, Xerox the following page before filling in blank spaces:

34

INSTITUTION AND AGENCY NOTIFICATION LIST

* NAME _____
  ADDRESS _____
  TELEPHONE NR. _____
** DATE AND TIME AGENCY NOTIFIED _____
  REQUEST BY AGENCY OR INSTITUTION _____
  _____
  DATE ACTION COMPLETED _____

+++++

* NAME _____
  ADDRESS _____
  TELEPHONE NR. _____
** DATE AND TIME AGENCY NOTIFIED _____
  REQUEST BY AGENCY OR INSTITUTION _____
  _____
  DATE ACTION COMPLETED _____

+++++

* NAME _____
  ADDRESS _____
  TELEPHONE NR. _____
** DATE AND TIME AGENCY NOTIFIED _____
  REQUEST BY AGENCY OR INSTITUTION _____
  _____
  DATE ACTION COMPLETED _____

+++++

* NAME _____
  ADDRESS _____
  TELEPHONE NR. _____
** DATE AND TIME AGENCY NOTIFIED _____
  REQUEST BY AGENCY OR INSTITUTION _____
  _____
  DATE ACTION COMPLETED _____

+++++

* NAME _____
  ADDRESS _____
  TELEPHONE NR. _____
** DATE AND TIME AGENCY NOTIFIED _____
  REQUEST BY AGENCY OR INSTITUTION _____
  _____
  DATE ACTION COMPLETED _____

+++++

* NAME _____
  ADDRESS _____
  TELEPHONE NR. _____
**DATE AND TIME AGENCY NOTIFIED _____
  REQUEST BY AGENCY OR INSTITUTION _____
  _____
  DATE ACTION COMPLETED _____

+++++

INSTITUTION AND AGENCY NOTIFICATION LIST

* NAME _____
ADDRESS _____
TELEPHONE NR. _____
** DATE AND TIME AGENCY NOTIFIED _____
REQUEST BY AGENCY OR INSTITUTION _____
_____
DATE ACTION COMPLETED _____
+++++

* NAME _____
ADDRESS _____
TELEPHONE NR. _____
** DATE AND TIME AGENCY NOTIFIED _____
REQUEST BY AGENCY OR INSTITUTION _____
_____
DATE ACTION COMPLETED _____
+++++

* NAME _____
ADDRESS _____
TELEPHONE NR. _____
**DATE AND TIME AGENCY NOTIFIED _____
REQUEST BY AGENCY OR INSTITUTION _____
_____
DATE ACTION COMPLETED _____
+++++

* NAME _____
ADDRESS _____
TELEPHONE NR. _____
** DATE AND TIME AGENCY NOTIFIED _____
REQUEST BY AGENCY OR INSTITUTION _____
_____
DATE ACTION COMPLETED _____
+++++

* NAME _____
ADDRESS _____
TELEPHONE NR. _____
** DATE AND TIME AGENCY NOTIFIED _____
REQUEST BY AGENCY OR INSTITUTION _____
_____
DATE ACTION COMPLETED _____
+++++

* NAME _____
ADDRESS _____
TELEPHONE NR. _____
**DATE AND TIME AGENCY NOTIFIED _____
REQUEST BY AGENCY OR INSTITUTION _____
_____
DATE ACTION COMPLETED _____
+++++

EMPLOYMENT
DATA SHEET NR _____ TO GFMS ENCLOSURE - FOUR

1. PURPOSE OF THIS FORM: a. Provides annuitant with a record of employment, promotions or change of employment. b. Provide survivor with a complete record on where and how to report annuitant's death. c. Provides survivor with record of survivor benefits if so elected. d. To expedite claim for survivor annuities where applicable. e. To attach supporting documents pertaining to this one particular employment.

2. KEEPING TRACK OF EMPLOYMENT: For record purposes, at above heading, enter the numerical number "1" to identify it as Data Sheet Nr. __1__. If you have previous records of employment, you may want to briefly enter the information in the comments section of page 38 or refer to the file of previous records of employment. From now on each time you change employment firms, fill in a new employment data sheet, number it in sequence and attach supporting documents. <u>Before filling in, make three copies for future use.</u>

3. FIRM, AGENCY AND PERSONAL DATA:

Annuitant's Full Name: _____

Last four of SSN: _____

Current Address: _____

_____

Name and Place of Current Employment: _____

(Name of Company, firm or agency)

_____

(Complete Address and Telephone Number)

_____

Date employment started: _____

Starting salary or wages: _____

Current salary or wages: _____ Date: _____

(Update every six-months)

Name of Manager or Supervisor: _____ / _____

(Contact in case of emergency)   (Telephone number)

Do you have HEALTH, LIFE and Financial Saving Plan through your employment firm or agency? If yes, to any or all of the plans, give name of person or agent that handles your pay and saving investment: _____

(Name of Person or Agent)

_____

(Complete Address and Telephone Number)

Is this period of employment Full Time Career?_____, Full Time Temporary? _____ Temporary? _____, or Part-Time? _____.

EMPLOYMENT DATA SHEET, CONTINUED

Are you attending college or technical school to further advance you into a career job? Yes _____ No _____ Name of school or college _____
_____
_____

Date employment ended: _____ Reason? _____
_____
_____

When changing positions, jobs for promotions or advancements within same employment firm, indicate changes in the comments section. If you leave one firm to work else where in another firm or company, annotate above the date ended and reason. Keep only current employment sheet at enclosure Nr. Four. Remove the old record employment data sheet along with any supporting documents in their document protector and add it at the very end of your GFMS binder or file it in accordance with instructions in enclosure Nr. Ten.

COMMENTS: _____
_____
_____
_____
_____
_____
_____
_____
_____
_____
_____
_____
_____
_____
_____
_____
_____
_____
_____
_____
_____

"Continue on separate lined white paper if needed."

RETIREMENT
DATA SHEET NR _____ TO GFMS ENCLOSURE - FOUR

1. PURPOSE OF THIS FORM: a. Provide annuitant with a record of retirement. b. Provide survivor with a complete record on where and how to report annuitant's death. c. Provide survivor with record of retirement for survivor benefits. d. To expedite claim for survivor annuities.

2. RECORDS OF RETIREMENT: When you reach retirement age, you will receive acknowledgement of some kind, be it in form of a letter, certificate, orders and notice of financial annuity, etc. In some form or another you will have documentation to verify your retirement. If you get partial or full disability, prior to reaching reduced or full disability age, you must protect and file these documents here with your retirement data sheet. In case of your demise, these records are of utmost importance to your survivor for, filing survivor claims based on the choices you made while still living.

For example, lets say you served your country and retired from the military service. You now have the documents of your first retirement. Fill out a Retire-ment Data Sheet and annotate it as Nr. __1__. Place the data sheet in document protectors as well as supporting documents and file them at Enclosure Nr. FOUR. Perform the same procedure as above for any subsequent retirements. Before filling in, make a copy for reproducing as needed.

3. RETIREMENT AND PERSONAL DATA:

Retiree's (annuitant) Full Name: _____

Last four of SSN: _____

Current Address: _____

_____

Name and Place of Retirement Agency: _____
(Name of Company, Firm or Agency)

_____
(Complete Address and Telephone Number)

_____

Assigned Agency or Civilian Firm Claim Number: _____
(Example: VA, CSA, CSI, OWCP or SSAN Nr.)

Elected Beneficiary: _____
(Full Name, Complete Address and Telephone Number -- If available, FAX & E-mail)

_____

_____

RETIREMENT DATA SHEET, CONTINUED

For health and life insurance policies or coverage, refer to Enclosure - Five.

Is this retirement accredited to a career under one agency, firm or company listed above? Yes ____, No ____. If no, please explain: _____
_____
_____
_____

Date Career Employment Started: _____

Effective Date of Retirement: _____

Did you elect full survivor benefits for your spouse under this retirement? Yes ____, No ____. If you checked "no", what percentage did you select? 50% _____ ,25% ____? If none were selected, (this sometimes happens) did you discuss it with your current spouse? Perhaps you were still single or became a widow/widower after your first retirement? If you married or re-married, discuss your retirement benefits with your current spouse. Remember, you have a limited time (less than 60-days) to claim and file for new spouse survivor benefits after your marriage. It is best to contact your retirement agency immediately after marriage to start survivor benefit and begin deducting costs from your annuity.

4. ANNOTATING COMMENTS: Should you or your spouse have any unusual circumstances concerning your retirement not already listed above, write them down here, no matter how insignificant you think it may be: _____
_____
_____
_____
_____
_____
_____
_____
_____
_____
_____
_____
_____
_____
_____

"Continue on separate white lined paper if needed."

REPORTING DEATH OF ANNUITANT
NOTIFICATION LETTER TO EMPLOYER OR RETIREMENT
AGENCY/FIRM

Survivor may use this letter of notification simply by cutting off this upper part, make as many copies as needed, filling in the blanks and mailing to the firm or agency requiring notice of death or use as a sample to write own letter.

✂ ---

Date: _____, Claimant's Telephone Nr. _____

From: _____

_____

_____

To: _____

_____

_____

Dear Sir or Madam,

I am sorry to inform you that my _____,_____, has
                                   (Husband/Wife)   (Full Name of Deceased)
passed away. I have enclosed a certified copy of the death certificate for your information.

To help you locate this case file, I am providing the following information:
Date and place of birth: _____
Social Security Nr: _____
Claim/File Number: _____
                       (EXAMPLE: VA, CSA, CSI, OWCP, SSAN or other firm claim number)

I have arranged to return the last annuity check or in case of direct deposit, the last annuity funds, by notifying my bank or credit union.

I ask that you please send me the forms needed to apply for survivor benefits and life insurance claim. If you have any questions concerning my claim, please call me at the telephone number listed above. Thank you for your help.

Sincerely,

_____
(Survivor/Claimant's Signature)

One Enclosure: Certified copy of death certificate

REPORTING DEATH OF ANNUITANT'S <u>SPOUSE</u>
NOTIFICATION LETTER TO RETIREMENT AGENCY/FIRM

Annuitant may use this letter of notification by cutting off this upper part, make as many copies as needed, filling in the blanks and mail to the firm or agency requiring notice of death or use as a sample to write own letter.

✂ --

Date: _____,Annuitant's Telephone Nr. _____

From: _____
          _____
          _____

To: _____
          _____
          _____

Dear Sir or Madam,

I am sorry to inform you that my _____, _____, has
                             (Husband/Wife)   (Full Name of Deceased)
passed away. I have enclosed a certified copy of the death certificate for your information.

I am a retiree/employee through your agency, following is the information for locating my file:

My claim number is: _____
                   (EXAMPLE: VA, CSA, CSI, OWCP, SSAN or other claim number)
My D.O.B.:___/___/___, P.O.B.: _____ SSAN: ____/___/____
(Date of Birth)   Mo Day Yr   (Place of Birth)   (City and State)   (Social Security Number)

My Spouse's SSAN: ____/___/____, and D.O.B.: _____

Upon my retirement, I elected a reduced annuity to provide a survivor's benefit for my _____, a benefit that is now no longer needed. Please restore my annuity to the
(Husband/wife)
full unreduced life rate.

•   Continued on backside:

43

REPORTING DEATH OF ANNUITANT'S SPOUSE Continued;

I _____ have other dependents who are covered by my retirement agency health
   (DO or DO NOT)
insurance, please _____change my coverage _____.
        (DO NOT or DO)   (FROM "FAMILY" or TO "SELF ONLY")

Please send me the necessary form to change my life insurance beneficiary. It is very important that I do this as soon as possible.

Should my records reflect that I am paying life insurance coverage on my spouse, please send me the necessary claims form for filing claim.

If applicable, and should my spouse be receiving retirement or social security annuity check, I will return the last check or the funds in the amount of last check if already cashed. If in case of direct deposit, I will notify the bank or credit union to return the last annuity funds deposited.

If you have any questions concerning this letter, please call me at the telephone number listed at top of letter.

Thank you for your assistance in making these necessary changes and I will be waiting for the requested changes and forms.

Sincerely,

_____
    (Annuitant's Signature)

One Enclosure: Certified copy of death certificate

44

ENCLOSURE - FIVE

© 2002

SUBJECT: Life and Health Insurance Policy/Coverage.

1. PURPOSE: To record and keep policies where survivor can easily find them.

2. ONLY ACTIVE POLICIES: At this enclosure and following page annotate <u>all active</u> life and health insurance policies and coverage. Write the name of company, address, telephone number and where original policy or certificate of insurance is kept. If you have old, inactive policies (invalid) in your files, send them back or destroy them. No need to confuse them with <u>your active policies.</u>

Policies and certificates of insurance vary in size and some can be too large for filing in this guide. If they fit in a document protector, by all means attach them to this enclosure. See Enclosure - Ten for filing instructions.

Review your insurance policies/coverage as changes occur or on a yearly basis to insure they meet your family needs. If you're employed by an established firm or agency, your insurance needs are probably met and payments are already being made through payroll deduction.

When you retire from your career employment, arrange to have all your insurance and health coverage payments made directly from your annuity. Most banking facilities will gladly arrange insurance payments directly from your savings or checking account. In the latter, you must keep good record to insure sufficient funds are maintained available in your accounts to cover payments and perhaps small service fees if applicable. As a precaution, always check your monthly bank statements to insure your payments to insurance companies are being made. Check with your banking facility and ask if they offer these type services.

3. LIFE AND HEALTH INSURANCE LIST:

Name of Insurance Company	Address & Telephone Number	Where Kept

LIFE AND HEALTH INSURANCE LIST, Continued:

Name of Insurance Company	Address & Telephone Number	Where Kept

ENCLOSURE - SIX

© 2002

SUBJECT: Banking Facilities and Your Financial Status.

PURPOSE: a. To offer annuitant recommended methods of controlling his/her monies and maximizing savings. b. To help annuitant prepare his/her spouse and family's financial foundation.

1. PROTECTING YOUR LIVELIHOOD: You have heard it countless times, keep sufficient funds in your savings account to cover you for six (6) months equal to your current living expenses. For example; from your employer, you receive $1,600.oo per month ($400.oo per week) after taxes and deductions. The total, amount of $1,600.oo x six-months = $9,600.oo as reserve savings for living expenses.

Should you get laid off from work, first file for unemployment benefits for living expense money until you find other employment. Use your reserve savings only as a last resort. Don't procrastinate in seeking other work, you worked hard to save your reserve saving. After returning to work, make up the money used while out of work as soon as possible, you never know when hard times will recur. Do not count on the economy or market trends to secure your job or career - anything can happen to cause an upset in this problematic world. The best advice is to budget, save and make wise investments with your money. All library attendants can help you find excellent books on how to control money.

You already know that your banking facility is the best source for controlling your money when you seek and use it wisely. Call your bank's President or Vice President, ask to meet them in person and ask them to assign you an financial advisor even if you don't have much money. Be honest, positive and sincere and tell them you want all non-essential debts paid off in their entirety, either through consolidation or their advise and guidance. Ask your advisor to help you set-up a savings and investment plan. Some other steps you can take to free yourself from money worries are to manage your "essential" debts better. Essential debts include only, your property/home and one automobile for transportation needs. Arrange for your children's education, plan your financial future "now" rather than later, and protect what you have saved and <u>keep</u> on <u>saving</u>. Ask yourself each time you go to purchase an item, "is this absolutely necessary?" If not, put that money you would have spend into a piggy bank and at the end of each week deposit the moneys in your reserve savings.

If your married, make appointments to meet with your banking advisor and bring your spouse with you. Your children ten-years and older should accompany you so they can learn about money responsibilities and saving. Ask your children to be respectful, listen while in with your advisor and to save their questions until your away form public audience. Teach your children through positive guidance, to save twenty-five percent (25%) of their allowance, babysitting or other earnings while young. In time, they will ask you about opening their own savings account at the bank, it's a learning process.

If you're a young, single person and working for your own money, ask your parents to attend the first couple of meetings with you. Your bank's advisors would be impressed with your serious and interesting approach to better your financial status if you bring your family to the meetings.

2. ACTION and COMMITMENT REFLECT POWERFUL RESULTS.

Now you can take full control of your money for taking care of yourself and your family. Read the recommended method of actions and commitment to begin your journey to financial stability and freedom from credit card and loan companies. Use the income and expenditure worksheets to determine your present financial status along with the methods to organize your files. Seek moral support and advice from your spouse and or parents.

Think about, how your loved ones will live after your gone? To prepare for your survivor is a difficult task and a subject nobody wants to discuss. Face it head-first without hesitation and get this behind you. Everybody should take action for their own responsibilities.

   a. WHO NEEDS TO TAKE ACTIONS? If you, the annuitant find yourself short of money before the next paycheck then, you are a candidate for better control of your own income and spending. This enclosure of your GFMS is your guide to help you organize and succeed. If you find yourself short of time because of your work, ask your spouse, parents or a friend, to help with organizing your records for you, don't be shy.

   b. WHEN CAN YOU START? Start now by keeping record of total expenditures. Locate all your income, retirement and annuity statements. Review the Income, expense worksheets and tips at end of this enclosure and begin filling in figures and information soon as possible. Time is of essence.

   c. WHAT MUST YOU DO AND HOW MUST YOU PROCEED? First (TAKE ACTION) you must organize all your statements by type income and by date with the most current on top. Separate them by year and staple them together and place them in labeled file folder. See Enclosure - Ten.

Every year thereafter, and upon completion of your Federal and State income taxes, review your income statements to insure they match your W-2 and 1099-R statements. In addition, also review your income totals against your Social Security earning statements, insure accredits match.

Annotate on your copy of the income tax files that you agree or disagree with the figures and write or print your initials as a reminder. If you find a mistake, take the necessary action to correct it. You may (if you feel comfortable) shred or destroy all **income** statements four years and older after insuring you reviewed the records for past three-years. **Federal and State income tax returns;** All tax payers should keep their Federal and State income tax files for a minimum of seven (7) years, if your wealthy, keep them ten (10) years or more.

d. COMMITMENT; Commit yourself and continue keeping record of your income and expenditures on a monthly basis for twelve-months.

After the first two months, the record will show if you are spending too much or perhaps overspending. Begin looking for unnecessary spending, start cutting back where you can and what you do save, deposit immediately in your savings account. Don't spend any of the money you are saving from expenditure reductions, instead, use the money to built up your reserve living funds. After organizing your financial files and completing the worksheets, call and make the appointment with your bank's president or vice president as mentioned in page one above. Don't look back, keep squeezing for addition to your savings. When the first year is over, decide if you need to continue working on expenditure worksheet. If you were successful in reducing your spending by twenty-percent (20%) or more, you may stop recording your expenditures. Whenever you feel the spending is getting out of hand, resume the procedure on your worksheet for no less than one-year increments.

e. WHERE MUST YOU KEEP RECORDS OF FINANCIAL MATERS? Always keep your records of financial matters along with your GFMS binder in a safe or filing cabinet under lock and key. Remember, these are sensitive documents and files.

3. RECORDING YOUR INCOME; First, record all the income you have coming after taxes so you can match exactly with what you have going out. On the income worksheet below, write down all your income your fairly certain will continue coming in for more than one year. If your fully employed but planning to retire within six-months, calculate your retirement income and use those figures as your income. Use these last few months before retirement as an adjusting transition period while you still have extra money while employed.

It is difficult to adjust to a limited retirement income after you retire than if you adjust before you retire. If you have other income, such as part-time/ temporary work and expecting to last less than one year, do not include this figure as income. Instead use the part-time income only to purchase "NEED" items or pay off high interest bearing credit cards. Be honest with yourself, you have to know for the "long term" if you have the money coming in to pay for what is going out when living on a reduced budget or on retirement income.

INCOME WORKSHEET	Yearly Income
EMPLOYMENT ONLY YOUR INCOME - After taxes /	
SOCIAL SECURITY INCOME	
STATE / FEDERAL CIVIL SERVICE RETIREMENT	
MILITARY / VA RETIREMENT	
DISABILITY INCOME (Other than Soc. Scty, Civil Svc or	
PENSION INCOME	
RENTAL INCOME	
PREDICTABLE, AUTHORIZED & CONTRACT BONUSES	
TRUST FUND / DIVIDEND INCOME	
PRIVATE BUSINESS INCOME (Must be established to qualify)	
RA, TSP, 401-k, ETC INCOME (If more than one, combine sum)	
OTHER INCOME (Do Not include income from your spouse or	

TOTAL: --- $_____

Monthly average income: (divide total by 12 & enter here) ----------- $_____

4. TIPS FOR SAVING MONEY. The following is a sample list of actions you can take to easily trim unnecessary expenditures. In addition, start by creating a list that will fit your style or category of living and work on reducing, trimming or eliminating spending.

ACTION	*YEARLY SAVINGS*
PURCHASE USED CAR RATHER THAN NEW-save on ins. and DMV reg.+	$ 1,000.00
PERFORM OWN CAR MAINT.-lub, oil, filters, plugs, tire rota, winter prep	$ 770.00
PARK CAR -Kids can use bicycle or motor scooter for short dist errands.	$ 300.00
CARPOOL - fuel, average savings; $65.00 per month	$ 780.00
ACCOUNTANT FEES - Do taxes with computer program and save	$ 500.00
MOW YOUR OWN LAWN - average savings	$ 700.00
BUY NON-PARISHABLE GOODS BY THE CASE - at case lot sales	$ 500.00
TOTAL savings in seven categories:	**$ 4,550.00**

EXPENDITURE WORKSHEET

INSTRUCTIONS: 1. Using this worksheet, record the amount that you spent monthly in each category. If there is a category relevant to you that is not listed in the worksheet, then add it in the blank space at the bottom. Start saving receipts and keeping track of your expenditures on the first day of the following month which you are presently in. For example; your now in September -- you want to begin tracking on October 1st through 31st so you have a full month to record. Total your expenditures "by category" for the month of October then enter that totals under the October column. Repeat this process for all twelve months.

2. After all the categories for the twelve months are complete, total each category and enter in the "Yearly total by category"

3. Then, for each category, divide the "Total Yearly by Category" figure by 12. This will give you how much you spend per month on average for that category. Write the figure in the column "Monthly Average by Category.

4. Next, add together all the "Monthly Average by Category" figures and write this at the bottom of the worksheet where it reads; **"TOTAL monthly average going out for all categories:" $ _____**. This will tell you the average that it costs to live each month for all categories. Be aware that you are working with averages. If your last figure average is $2,800.oo, you will notice that some months you will spend less and other months more. In the end, the $2,800.oo figure is the number you need to work with. Due to limited space, **use only whole dollar figures.** Fifty-cents or more, go up, .49-cents or less go down.

CATEGORY	JAN/	FEB/	MAR/	APR/	MAY/	JUN/	JUL/	AUG/	SEP/	OCT/	NOV/	DEC/	Yearly Total by Category	Monthly Aver. by Category
Alimony, child														
Auto expenses, all														
Bank, credit Un														
Books,														
Burglar alarm +														
Cable, TV,														
Tobacco,														
Cloths, shoes etc														
PC, Software, supl														
Credit Cards, loans														
Donation, tip etc														
Dry clean, laundry														
Video, entertain														
Heat, oil & gas														
Food/restaurant														
Garbage pickup														

Continued on next page:

EXPENDITURE WORKSHEET, Continued

CATEGORY	JAN/	FEB/	MAR/	APR/	MAY/	JUN/	JUL/	AUG/	SEP/	OCT/	NOV/	DEC/	Yearly /	Monthly
Garden, yard, lawn														
Gas & elec. Utility														
Gifts, all categories														
Health & beauty														
Hobbies, all categories														
Home Insurance														
Home maint. fees														
House clean, in/out														
Income taxes - all														
Ins. Life & health														
Jewelry														
Job, training & education														
Kid's school expenses														
Legal, acct. fees														
Lottery, casino +														
Medical, dental, optometry														
Miscellaneous														
Mortgage or rent														
Pools and spa														
Postage, mail, all														
Property, home tax														
Safety & security														
Sporting events, all														
Tele, cell & internet														
Tolls & parking fees														
Vacation, camp, tours														
Veterinarian Svc														
Water for irrigation														

TOTAL monthly average going out for all categories: $_____ /_____
  Continue on separate white lined paper if adding more items.

ENCLOSURE - SEVEN

© 2002

SUBJECT: Credit Institutions and Your Debts.

1. PURPOSE: a. To record all current/active personal loans you may have existing in any dollar amount. b. To file existing promissory notes or loan payment contracts for easy reference and monitoring. c. To monitor your progress in paying off your personal loan debts. d. To make you aware that when you see the big picture of how much you owe, that you'll work harder to clear up all your personal loans, should you have any.

2. RESPONSIBILITY to YOUR FAMILY and LOVED ONES. How often do you think of the unexpected turns in life? What do you think would happen if you suddenly come down with a serious illness and your doctor told you that you had a short time to live? Would you think of the financial conditions you are about to leave your loved ones saddled with, good or bad? Having a bundle of money or not, a good paying job or not, will not help your family if your in debt while still here. It is after your death that the financial chaos strike. It will be hard enough for your family to bear the grief of your illness or death. Just think of the pain they would go through. So please do not let them face those financial difficulties and responsibilities you could have taken care of while you were alive and in good health.

By taking action, committing and reminding yourself to what is important in this life, what is important to you and who you are as a loving and caring father, mother, son, brother or sister, you will succeed in your endeavors.

Enclosure six gives you the tools to work towards financial control and freedom of debt, use it well. Don't wait the full year before you start reducing and clearing your debts. The spending trends begin showing up after recording the first two-months. By completing the rest of this GFMS, these obstacles and tasks will rapidly start clearing away, relieving stress, doubts, anxiety and tension.

3. LISTING YOUR PERSONAL DEBTS. All debts are personal debts if you signed the agreement to pay them. On the following page list all your personal debts and attach the promise note or loan agreement until you pay that loan in full. Upon receiving your final receipt or statement showing your loan or note is paid in full, staple it to the promissory note or loan agreement and file it in your personal files, see Enclosure - Ten. Next refer to Enclosure - Seven, pages 54 and 55 and redline through loan or debt and indicate date paid in full.

Be sure you have a receipt or statement from the loan company indicating your loan is paid in full. Keep your receipts on file for a minimum of two-years for proof of payment in full and for itemized tax deduction.

4. ANTICIPATED DEBT? If you are thinking about a large purchase, be it a washer and dryer or a car, start saving now and hold off purchase as long as possible. Meanwhile, shop around for lowest price and ask for ninety (90) day payment plan <u>without interest.</u> If your in need of a car and don't already have one, buy a used car as starters. It will save you two to three thousand or more dollars. You can always trade it in for a new car after you have paid your other debts or keep it for work and save miles on your new car. Saves on insurance!!

5. ALL DEBTS. For real estate, home mortgage/deeds and vehicle registration or titles, see enclosure - nine. If you owe money on these purchases, enter figures here. Continue on separate sheet if needed.

Real Estate/ Home		Purchase Price	Yearly Tax	Payment	$ Balance	Date
☑	/					
	/					
	/					
	/					

Car Make, Year	Purchase Price	Lic. Reg.	Payment	$ Balance	Inspections

Credit Card/Type	Yearly Fee	Int. Rate	Payment	$ Balance	Purpose

Name all Other Loans	Date	Int. Rate	Payment	$ Balance	Purpose

GFMS, ENCL - 7 "DEBTS" Continued:

Name all Other Loans	Date	Int. Rate	Payment	$ Balance	Purpose

TOTAL DEBTS on real estate and or home> $_____

TOTAL DEBTS on all transportation vehicles> $_____

TOTAL DEBTS on all credit cards> $_____

TOTAL DEBTS all other loans> $_____

COMBINED TOTAL OF ALL DEBTS: $_____

QUESTION? Are you just making ends meet or maybe over committed?
SUGGESTION; Read again, page - 1 of enclosure - six. Make that appointment with the President of your banking facility, inform your spouse, children or parents, get nicely dressed and go petition your Bank President to help you..

Prepare your presentation by taking your GFMS and presenting your honest commitment to eliminate your debts through a consolidated loan or through "his professional advise."

Use next page to prepare an outline of your presentation or just simply to make notes to remind you of the actions you need and must take to make your goal a reality. Don't give up, if at first you do not succeed - try again. Remember, where there is a will, there is a way!!

MY NOTES

ENCLOSURE - EIGHT

© 2002

SUBJECT: Retirement Investments and Savings.

1. PURPOSE: a. To record and control the accountability of all your money be it in cash or other investments. b. Saving for in case of hard times (six-times your monthly earnings) and for your children's education. c. Saving to buy with cash and not on credit. d. Saving for large purchases' such as land, home, or automobile. e. Preparing ahead and avoiding harsh and financial difficulty for your spouse, family or loved one for when you are no longer here.

2. GENERAL: Only by planning your estate do you exercise control over who or how much your beneficiary will benefit. Planning also gives you the opportunity to exclude anyone you wish from receiving a part or any of your estate except that State' Laws give your surviving spouse the right to share your estate. This share varies from State to State. It is always wise to see your lawyer before making decisions on financial appropriations of your estate.

3. RECORDING YOUR RETIREMENT INVESTMENTS: At enclosure-six, you recorded your income and expenditures to expose your financial status. It recommended methods of controlling your expenditures to your income and advice on helping you how to get out of debt and save more money. At enclosure-seven, you listed all your debts.

At this enclosure, record all your retirement investments you may already have. These monetary properties include; trust, property and earnings, insurance policies, individual retirement accounts (IRA, all categories), income or thrift savings plans, stocks, savings bonds and property held in joint tenancy with right of survivorship. If you don't have any retirement investments, talk with your bank financial advisor about starting an investment now.

These monetary retirement investments all need to be listed here for your survivor since retirement benefits don't go through probate. Individual retirement accounts (IRAs) will provide a <u>ready means of cash</u> for your survivor when you die. If you have a trust and your married, make sure your primary beneficiary is your spouse and not the trust. Trust can be second beneficiary.

If you are already retired, refer to enclosure-four where you recorded your work/career related retirements and annuities.

Then, if your drawing annuities from your listed retirement investments, insure you also record them at enclosure - four by filling out the retirement data sheet.

4. LIST OF YOUR RETIREMENT INVESTMENTS:

Type Investment	Name, Address, Telephone Nr. of Institution	Date Started	Current $ Value	Date Recorded

5. READY CASH SAVINGS: I encourage you to built-up your six-months unemployed savings as suggested in paragraph -1 of enclosure -six. Ask your bank advisor how you can invest this money for higher dividend returns and still be able to withdraw without fee or penalty if you may need this money without notice. If you are not yet fully retired and are still working, It would be wise to invest your saving in a Roth IRA without locking in your savings for long term. Ask your advisor about the details of a Roth-IRA account. You'll like what you hear!

58

ENCLOSURE - NINE

© 2002

SUBJECT: Real Estate, Transportation and Equipment.

1. PURPOSE: a. To record and account for all valuable tangible properties. b. To record the purchase price and current resale value. c. To Establish ready reference for your survivor. d. And to attach ownership and supporting documents.

2. RECORDING AND ACCOUNTING: Record all your tangible and valuable properties in the following blank columns for your survivor. Keep your listing current (in pencil) as you purchase, sell and replace your properties. Attach all supporting documents, such as vehicle titles or registrations, home or real estate deeds or mortgage papers and record or receipts of payments in full on all your business or farm equipment.

3. LIST OF YOUR PROPERTIES:

REAL-ESTATE

Property List and Address or Location	Purchase Price & Date	Payment If Financed	Current Balance	Resale Value	Date Recorded

" PERSONAL" TRANSPORTATION;
AIRPLANE, AUTOMOBILES, TRUCKS, MOTORCYCLES and SNOWMOBILES

Property List and Address or Location	Purchase Price & Date	Payment If Financed	Current Balance	Resale Value	Date Recorded

"" BUSINESS "" TRANSPORTATION AND EQUIPMENT; AIRPLANE, AUTOMOBILES, TRUCKS, MOTORCYCLES, SNOWMOBILES, ALL MAJOR OFFICE EQUIPMENT, ALL FARM EQUIPMENT and MACHINERY

Property List and Address or Location	Purchase Price & Date	Payment If Financed	Current Balance	Resale Value	Date Recorded

"BUSINESS" CONTINUATION SHEET

Property List and Address or Location	Purchase Price & Date	Payment If Financed	Current Balance	Resale Value	Date Recorded

ENCLOSURE - TEN

© 2002

SUBJECT: Documents, Files and Disposition.

1. PURPOSE: a. To list additional and or bulky file documents that support and directly relate to your GFMS. b. To list your personal and family files, their location and disposition. c. To list location of medical and dental records. d. To establish ready reference for your survivor.

2. **FILES:** Keeping your document files in good order will save your survivor much work and expenses when the time comes to settle your estate. Your executor or survivor can spend hundreds of dollars, days, weeks and sometimes months to search for and obtain legal and personal papers especially if you own a business. Consider the numerous hours of search, travel, lawyer fees plus cost of obtaining the documents to settle your estate after you are gone.

Keeping your documents and files in good order is your responsibility. Please, don't leave this burden to your spouse, parents or partner.

3. **SAFES AND CONTAINERS:** Bank deposit boxes, home safes and file containers are all a good source of security to certain extent. Security is only as good as can be afforded and this all depends on your standard of living. Use your own judgment but, first consider the accessibility to your files as if your had to settle your own estate. It will be great when you complete your GFMS and file it in your home safe which you have a key and combination to. This is what your survivor and executor would like to know, have access to keys, the combination and find all necessary documents in your GFMS binder after your demise. Help them now, coordinate this matters with your spouse, executor, parents or partner.

4. **IMPORTANT FILES AND DISPOSITION:** Other important files are your personal every day accessible files like, banking files, bills and record of payment, letter files, military service files, project or hobby files, etc. These files are important and some are probably historical like your family tree. Keep your GFMS files locked in a separate drawer or separate safe. Review your GFMS
quarterly and make necessary changes as they occur.

Should you have a business, operating in or away from your home, <u>do not</u> keep or file your GFMS within any of business files or containers. You don't want any body unauthorized looking through your GFMS under any circumstances.

Purge or review all your files every three-months to rid of expired, old or no longer useful papers and files. When you have orderly files and you let them accumulate (pile up) eventually you will begin shuffling through piles of paper to find what your looking for. Label your folder files neat and legibly and separate folders by major subject or labeled file dividers. For example; first file is a DIVIDER, labeled: BANK/FINANCE followed by a FILE FOLDER Subtitled; Checking and Saving Acct., next file folder number two Subtitled; Unemployed Savings Acct, file folder number three Subtitled; Car Loan, file folder number four Subtitled; Home & Property Mortgage, etc, etc. Your second DIVIDER can be: UTILITIES and FUELS; Followed by subtitled folders, etc, etc.

Gather your family around you or your parents, partner or trusted friend and explain that you need to organize your files and you need their help. Begin by making a list on lined paper with major title dividers. Leave ten spaces between each major title to list your folder titles as recommended in previous paragraph. Continue the process until you have listed all conceivable files you will need to organize a workable and controllable files system. Place your file dividers, followed by the file folders in the order of the most used folders up-front. Keep files that are least used to the back and bottom drawers.

5. MEDICAL and DENTAL RECORDS: It is very important for your survivor to know where your medical and dental records are kept and can be obtained. Why? If you happen to die in a natural disaster, a plane crash or even war, your remains if unrecognizable may need to be matched with your dental or medical records.

If you move often or if in military or government service, make a copy of your medical and dental records for your own safe keeping. Periodically update your copy of your medical and dental records. Lets say three-quarter through your work career, you experienced an work accident or devastating illness and you needed to apply for disability compensation or retirement. You will need a history of your medical treatments, conditions and perhaps proof that it was caused by previous work related illnesses or injuries. If you don't have copies readily available, it could take many weeks to obtain copies if at all. Meanwhile you have suspense dates to meet. Even if you do obtain copies of your records in a couple to three weeks, that means you would be pressed to prepare your application in a concise and complete manner. Any information you leave out concerning the history of medical conditions could cause you to be disapproved on your disability request.

Although you have a right to appeal, the burden of proof is still your responsibility. Stay prepared and make those copies now. Use a post-it-note and paste it here to remind you. Set a suspense date to get this project accomplished, the sooner the better. It's your right to have a copy.

64

When you make the copies of your medical and dental records, copy them in exact order as they are in your records. If your records are in a folder and there is information on the folder cover, copy that cover too. Be thorough and complete. Make copy updates each time you move or every January of the new year, which ever comes first.

6. **LIST OF YOUR FILES:** The list you make with the help of your family is the list you need to record here in the following graph. In case your files become disorganized in the future, you will be able to refer back here to get them back into organized order.

Title of Divider	Name of File "Subtitle"	Where is it Located: CD, Home Safe, cabinet (drawer Nr), desk, or bank	Disposition Control or Dispose

Title of Divider	Name of File "SUBTITLE"	Where is it Located: CD, Home Safe, cabinet (drawer Nr), desk or bank	Disposition Control or Dispose

SUBJECT: State and Federal Income Tax.

1. PURPOSE: a. To account for complete and filed State and Federal Income Tax for past three (3) years. b. To attach here, a copy of your latest state/federal income tax filed. c. To establish ready reference for your survivor.

2. TAXES: To advise about taxes and in what category you would fit in, is best left to your nearest IRS offices and tax advisors when it comes to income and estate taxes.

Basically, when a person dies, state tax codes and federal tax laws impose estate or death taxes on the decedent's possessions. Unless these taxes on the deceased's real and personal property are paid within a specified time, generally, nine months under the IRS code, a person's estate is subject to interest and penalty taxes and may not transfer to survivor, beneficiaries or heirs in accordance with decedent's wishes until these taxes, interest and penalty are paid.

You don't need to be afraid concerning estate taxes because there is an answer, a correct answer when you ask a qualified IRS agent or state and federal tax advisor. To best clear you conscious, make an appointment with your tax advisor and be prepared to ask all the questions concerning estate taxes. Bring your spouse, grown children or parents with you. Some of the questions you may ask about are; State Death Taxes, Pickup Taxes, Inheritance Taxes, Federal and State Income Taxes, Gift Taxes and Taxes on Survivor Annuities. Ask about how your surviving spouse would qualify for filing taxes for the year of your demise. What happens when your surviving spouse is an resident alien or perhaps an non-resident alien? Does it seem like a lot to you? Not really, it depend on your financial status or wealth. Ask for the guides, pamphlets and any additional advise you get from your advisor, then place them in document protector and attached them to this enclosure for use by your survivor.

Please, don't forget, each tax year to add your most current tax return filed, at this enclosure and remove the previous tax return file and place it in your inactive files (for taxes) folder. In addition, don't forget to review your income taxes to match your income vouchers/stubs and your social security yearly statement.

ENCLOSURE - TWELVE

© 2002

SUBJECT: Documents of Significant Value.

1. **PURPOSE:** a. To have certified copies readily available for your survivor. b. To inform survivor or executor where the original of documents are filed.

2. **BIRTH CERTIFICATE:** This document is very important in proof of citizenship, application for passport, verification of age and many government benefits. If you are married or single, keep five (5) certified copies at this enclosure along with original. Your survivor or executor will need to have access to both original and copies when needed. Always maintain control of your original birth certificate, keep it filed here.

Your birth certificate will be used by your spouse or beneficiary for application of survivor benefits; social security, veterans benefits, health and life insurance, military identification cards, VA dependent indemnity compensation claim and follow-up or pending disability claim if needed.

In case of adopted children, under eighteen-years of age or to 23 years if attending school of higher education, keep five (5) certified copies of their birth certificate along with five (5) certified copies of final authorization letter of adoption at this enclosure. File original adoption papers in a safe and secure location, refer to Enclosure - Ten. Insure spouse and executor know where originals are filed.

3. **MARRIAGE CERTIFICATE:**

A marriage certificate is proof of legal status of spouse in current marriage and in case of divorce, of previous marriages.

Survivor may be asked to submit a certified copy of their marriage certificate to prove their marital status to the deceased spouse in settlement of estate, life insurance claims or retirement annuities. The same applies if you happen to be divorced, paying alimony or child support as specified in the divorce decree. File original plus three (3) certified copies here.

4. **REPORT OF SEPARATION FROM ACTIVE DUTY, DD Form 214:**

At this enclosure keep a minimum of three (3) copies of annuitant's latest discharge and retirement discharge certificate, DD Form 214.

Copy number four is the only copy that designates type of discharge received. In addition, keep one copy of "all" other discharge certificates and discharge orders received in your military career at this enclosure.

Keep all "original" DD Form 214 certificates and discharge orders in their original folders in a separate and safe location such as a home safe, locked file cabinet or a bank safety deposit box. Some annuitants are very proud of their military career and service and display their certificates of discharge and awards at a selected location in their home. Caution; guard these and other documents with your social security number on them against identity theft.

5. DIVORCE DECREE AND PROPERTY SETTLEMENT (if applicable):

In case annuitant is divorced, keep the original divorce decree and any stipulation and order at this enclosure along with "three" (3) **court certified copies.** Label your original divorce decree so it is not mistaken for a copy. Do not release original.

Divorce decrees may be required for social security, VA benefits, child support, alimony or other property settlements.

6. PASSPORT:
If you have a passport, file it here until you need it for your travels outside the country where it was originally issued. Review your passport periodically to insure it is not expired. If you let your passport expire, it will cost you much more to renew and will take much longer to receive it.

7. CONTENTS IN YOUR WALLET OR PURSE:
Have you ever lost something that is very personal to you? Driver's license, credit carts, social security card, personal notes, "your hard earned money" or more? These are all items you may carry in your wallet or purse.

For those who have experienced their wallet or purse lost or stolen, anxiety kicks in, your blood pressure rises and your heart beat jumps to 180 bpm without doing exercise. What do you do? You back track all the steps you went through since the last time you seen it. Perhaps you find it perhaps not. But what if it has been stolen.

For your record, take all your important cards and other information out from your purse, wallet or billfold and lay them neatly on a Xerox and copy them. Turn them around exactly as they lay and copy the back side. Now you have a copy should you need to report the stolen items to the authorities, banks, etc.

God bless you and lead you to success in all your endeavors.

ABOUT THE AUTHOR

Jose Pineda was born in New Mexico. He attended school in Colorado and entered the U.S. Military at eighteen, completing twenty years of honorable service. His oversea assignments included Thailand, Vietnam, Ecuador and Germany. His specialty duties were those of Analyst and Photo/Imagery Interpreter included a two-years tenure as The First Sergeant of a company with over three hundred personnel in strength. After military service, he worked in civil service in Germany and The United States before retiring on disability. He is an inventor, innovator and now this is Jose's first book writing as an Author. Jose and his wife live in Germany.

www.ingramcontent.com/pod-product-compliance
Lightning Source LLC
Chambersburg PA
CBHW080433290526
45791CB00008BA/2484